I Played My Best for Him!

The Inspiring Stories Behind the Little Drummer Boy
and Other Christmas Favorites

OLAPEJU SIMOYAN

Copyright © 2024 by Olapeju Simoyan

All rights reserved. No portion of this book may be reproduced in any form without the express written permission of the author. The photographs in this book are the author's original works and may not be reproduced without permission.

Previous versions of the "Joy to the World" and "Feliz Navidad" essays have been published at: https://www.patheos.com/.

ISBN 979-8-9916570-0-6

Contents

Introduction	iv
The Little Drummer Boy	1
What Child is This?	5
Angels from the Realms of Glory	12
Joy to the World	18
Angels We Have Heard on High	24
O Holy Night	28
Mary's Boy Child	40
O Come, O Come, Emmanuel	44
It Came Upon the Midnight Clear	50
Silver Bells	56
I'll Be Home for Christmas	59
Silent Night	63
Feliz Navidad	79

Introduction

I have thoroughly enjoyed writing "I Played My Best for Him!" The inspiration came when I read the story behind "O Holy Night" at an event in December 2023. I thought it was fascinating and started looking into the stories behind other Christmas carols. Having just recorded *Peju Sings! The Little Drummer Boy and Other Christmas Favorites,* I was motivated to learn about the stories behind all thirteen songs on the album and compile them in a book! As with most other things, it ended up being a lot more work than I initially anticipated. Some details that have become "embedded" in a few of the stories are not verifiable (or have been debunked), so separating fact from fiction was a bit of a challenge. Some of the "facts" reported by sources that were considered reliable were contradicted by other sources. Regardless, the stories are full of intriguing details about people who have blessed us with the gift of Christmas music. In some cases, where there has been enough reason to doubt often-repeated aspects of the stories, I have included a brief discussion addressing the details that are in question. I have attempted, to the best of my ability, to present accurate versions of the stories. However, this is not intended to be an in-depth study of any of the subjects. It is meant to be an easy read, and the essay format allows for this.

Readers who are interested in further exploration can access the sources listed at the end of each essay.

These stories remind us that the composers and lyricists were regular people like us. It is interesting to think about what was going on in their lives at the time they created the songs. Another interesting observation is that several of the songs were not originally written in English and the words in the versions we sing are quite distinct from the original texts.

For example, the stories behind "Silent Night" and "O Holy Night," in addition to shedding light on the lives of the creators, highlight the challenges of translating a song from one language into another in a way that it can still be sung to the same tune without losing its meaning. Some would argue that meanings have been changed; so even though we sing the carols in English, we can learn a lot about the intent of the authors by examining the original texts.

One recurring theme was the role that many of these songs played during times of war. Soldiers on both sides stopped fighting temporarily and sang "Silent Night," *or was it "O Holy Night?"* You may have heard it was both. The "Silent Night" story is known as the "Christmas Truce of 1914," while the "O Holy Night" version may never have happened, since it can't be verified.

It isn't surprising that people would look to songs about peace on earth in times of war, but we can be inspired by these songs all year round. Christmas was probably far from Isaac Watts' mind as he meditated on Psalm 98 and penned the words that became

the song, "Joy to the World." Regardless of Watts' intent, this song has become one of the most beloved Christmas carols. The message of Christmas is one of hope, peace and goodwill and it is valid throughout the year.

The title of this book, "I Played My Best for Him," is from "The Little Drummer Boy," which tells the fictional story of a poor boy who came to see Christ, the newborn King, but had no gift to bring with him. He had no money but gave a gift that was priceless – he shared his talent by playing his drum. This is a powerful reminder that even with limited resources, we can make a positive impact on those around us by giving our time, talent and other resources, just like the Drummer Boy.

I hope you will be inspired and that you will enjoy reading this book as much as I enjoyed writing it.

Wishing you peace, joy and love, now and always.

The Little Drummer Boy

"The Little Drummer Boy" was written by Katherine Kennicott Davis, an American composer in 1941.

It was first published with the title "Carol of the Drum," and is believed to have been based on a Czech melody or inspired by a French Christmas carol. Some people believe that Davis wrote the song while trying to take a nap.

Composer - Katherine Kennicott Davis (1892 – 1980)

Katherine Kennicott Davis was born in St. Joseph, Missouri, to Jessie F. Barton and Maxwell Gaddis Davis. She eventually settled in Concord, Massachusetts, a town known for its New England transcendental poets. Her mother was a musician, which may partly explain her passion for folk music. She composed her first piece of music, "Shadow March," at the age of 15, and eventually composed more than 600 pieces of music. Davis studied music at Wellesley College in Massachusetts, winning the Billings Prize for composition. After graduation, she stayed on to teach music theory and composition. She also studied at the New England Conservatory of Music in Boston and with a private instructor in Paris.

Carol of the Drum

The Little Drummer Boy was written just before the Second World War. Times were hard and there was little money for Christmas presents, so it makes sense that Davis would have written a song about a child who had no money to buy a gift for a new-born King.

"Carol of the Drum" wasn't popular when it was first released, but that changed after it was recorded by the Trapp Family Singers in 1951 and further popularized by the Harry Simeone Chorale in 1958.

By 1962, "Little Drummer Boy" had been recorded over a hundred times and at the top of the charts five times. It has been recorded by various artists, including Bing Crosby and David Bowie (1977), Jonny Cash (1963) and Justin Bieber (2011). There are over 200 versions of "Little Drummer Boy" in seven languages.

A lasting legacy

Katherine Kenicott Davis never married, and she handled her publishing and finances by herself, something that was unusual for women in her time. In March of 1980, she wrote to one of

the companies that published her music, ECS Publishing, to tell them that she wanted to send them a setting of some of Isaac Watts' verses, called "Songs Abound." The publishers loved the piece, but unfortunately, Davis passed away before the project was completed.

The piece ended with these prophetic words:

Then let our songs abound
And every tear be dry;
We're marching through Emmanuel's ground
To fairer worlds on high.

Katherine Kennicott Davis died in 1980 at 87 and left all her royalties and proceeds to the music program at Wellesley College. Her legacy lives on through the music she created and no doubt, through the impact of her generosity. The words "I played my best for Him" in "The Little Drummer Boy," spoken by a little boy who had no money, serve to remind us that sometimes the greatest gifts are things that money can't buy. He had a drum, and he played his best for the new-born King. We, too, can use our gifts, resources and talents to make a difference in the world.

Sources

https://www.classicfm.com/discover-music/occasions/christmas/little-drummer-boy-carol-wartime-history/. August 3, 2024.

https://www.ecspublishing.com/composers/d/katherine-k-davis.html. Accessed August 3, 2024.

https://historybecauseitshere.weebly.com/katherine-davis-the-little-drummer-boy.html. Accessed August 3, 2024.

https://www.newspressnow.com/life/little-drummer-boy-written-by-st-joseph-native/article_8da7bd6e-1062-51d9-b307-e4dc536419d4.html. Accessed August 3, 2024.

What Child is This?

"What Child is This" was written by William Chatterton Dix around 1865.

Words - William Chatterton Dix (1837-1898)

William Chatterton Dix was born in England, to John and Sussanah Dix. John Dix was a surgeon who also happened to be a writer. John wrote the autobiography of Thomas Chatterton, a poet. The younger Dix took his father's advice to follow in the footsteps of the poet he had been named after.

William Chatterton Dix trained in the business world and became the manager of a marine insurance company in Glasgow, Scotland. He continued to write and was even accused of treating poetry as his passion and his job as a "side gig." As a young adult, he had a life-threatening illness and was bedridden for a protracted period. He became depressed and experienced a spiritual crisis during this time. This experience led him to become a man of devout faith. He eventually recovered, returned to work, and was inspired to write poetry and hymns with Christian themes, including "Alleluia, Sing to Jesus" and "As With Gladness Men of Old."

During Dix's time, Christmas was not celebrated the way it is today. Some churches even forbade any acknowledgment of Christmas, including decorations and gift-giving. The Puritans did not want pagan rituals to replace serious worship. Some churches held Christmas services but maintained that Christmas Day was for worship only. Given this backdrop, it is somewhat surprising that Dix was motivated to write about the first Christmas. His poem, written around 1865, tells the story of Christ's coming from the perspective of an observer. Various sources state that "What Child is This" was part of a longer poem, "The Manger Throne." A comparison of the texts suggests that a more likely explanation was that the song was inspired by the poem, rather than a part of it.

Music - Greensleeves

Dix's poem became well-known in the United States just as the Civil War was ending. Although it was used in church services and appeared in print, it was only after it was coupled with the "Greensleeves" tune that it became extremely popular. Registered in England in 1580, "Greensleeves" was a popular folk song, almost as popular as the national anthem. It was about a lover's rejection by Lady Greensleeves:

"Alas, my love, you do me wrong,
To cast me off discourteously.
For I have loved you well and long,
Delighting in your company.
"Greensleeves was all my joy

Greensleeves was my delight,
Greensleeves was my heart of gold,
And who but my Lady Greensleeves."

It is unclear who was responsible for pairing Dix's lyrics with the Greensleeves tune. Some historians believe that the melody was already popular in England at the time the song Greensleeves was registered. There have even been claims that King Henry VIII composed it, but a more likely explanation seems to be that it developed over an Italian dance bass, like several other melodies that came to England in the sixteenth century. Fortunately for Dix, he lived to see his poem become the popular Christmas carol, "What Child is This?"

John Stainer's arrangement of the song was featured in a collection titled "Christmas Carols Old and New" in 1871 and may have contributed to its popularity. Of the over forty hymns that Dix wrote, "What Child is This" has been the most enduring and is more popular in the United States than in the United Kingdom where it originated. Often associated with guitar solos, the melody is captivating whether it's performed by a choir, orchestra, or a capella.

Sources

Bradley, Ian (ed.) *The Penguin Book of Carols*, Penguin Books, 1999, pp. 381-383.

Collins, Ace. *Stories Behind the Best-Loved Songs of Christmas*, Zondervan, 2001, pp. 183-187.

Gant, Andrew. *Carols of Christmas: A Celebration of the Surprising Stories Behind Your Favorite Holiday Songs,* Thomas Nelson, 2015, pp. 393-394.

Mosteller, Angie. *Christmas Songs - Stories Behind the Classic Songs of Christmas*, 2010, pp. 113-115.

https://www.hymncharts.com/2022/11/16/what-child-is-this/. Accessed August 15, 2024.

What Child Is This? – Sermon Writer. Accessed August 15, 2024.

What Child is This?

1. What child is this, who, laid to rest,
   On Mary's lap is sleeping,
   Whom angels greet with anthems sweet
   While shepherds watch are keeping?
   This, this is Christ the King,
   Whom shepherds guard and angels sing;
   Haste, haste to bring Him laud,
   The babe, the son of Mary!

2. Why lies He in such mean estate
   Where ox and ass are feeding?
   Good Christian, fear: for sinners here
   The silent Word is pleading.
   Nails, spear shall pierce him through,
   The Cross be borne for me, for you;
   Hail, hail the Word Made Flesh,
   The babe, the son of Mary!

3. So bring Him incense, gold, and myrrh;
   Come, peasant, king, to own Him!
   The King of Kings salvation brings;
   Let loving hearts enthrone Him!
   Raise, raise the song on high!
   The virgin sings her lullaby.
   Joy! joy! for Christ is born,
   The babe, the son of Mary!

The Manger Throne

Like silver lamps in a distant shrine,
    The stars are sparkling bright
The bells of the city of God ring out,
    For the Son of Mary is born to-night.
The gloom is past and the morn at last
    Is coming with orient light.

Never fell melodies half so sweet
    As those which are filling the skies,
And never a palace shone half so fair
    As the manger bed where our Savior lies;
No night in the year is half so dear
    As this which has ended our sighs.

Now a new Power has come on the earth,
    A match for the armies of Hell:
A Child is born who shall conquer the foe,
    And all the spirits of wickedness quell:
For Mary's Son is the Mighty One
    Whom the prophets of God fortell.

The stars of heaven still shine as at first
    They gleamed on this wonderful night;
The bells of the city of God peal out
    And the angels' song still rings in the height;
And love still turns where the Godhead burns
    Hid in flesh from fleshly sight.

Faith sees no longer the stable floor,
    The pavement of sapphire is there
The clear light of heaven streams out to the world
    And the angels of God are crowding the air,
And heaven and earth, through the spotless birth
    Are at peace on this night so fair.

Angels from the Realms of Glory

"Angels from the Realms of Glory" was originally a poem written by James Montgomery. Church congregations started singing it after it was published in *The Christian Psalmist* and *The Christmas Box or New Year's Gift* (published by the Religious Tract Society).

Words - James Montgomery (1771-1854)

James Montgomery was born in 1771 in Irvine, Ayrshire, Scotland. His father was a Moravian pastor. James was sent to live at the Moravian seminary at Fulneck in Yorkshire at the age of six or seven when his parents went to Barbados as missionaries. Unfortunately, they never saw their son again, as they died there. Montgomery attended a Moravian school in England and had a love for poetry. He was a gifted writer, but this ended up distracting him from his schoolwork and he was eventually dismissed from school. He was sent to work as an apprentice to a baker but ended up running away. He eventually got a job as a clerk with Mr. Gales, the publisher of the *Sheffield Register* in 1792.

The newspaper was sympathetic towards the French Revolution and Gales eventually had to flee to France due to the threat of political persecution. Montgomery then took over, serving as editor for 31 years. He toned down the political rhetoric of the newspaper and changed its name to *Sheffield Iris,* while remaining concerned about issues of social justice.

Despite the changes, Montgomery was imprisoned twice in the 1790s, first for printing a song in support of the Bastille in the French Revolution, and for allegedly biased reporting on a reform riot in Sheffield. He continued to champion the cause of the oppressed, even while in prison.

At the age of 26, Montgomery published a collection of poems he had written during his time of incarceration, titled *Prison Amusements*. He produced approximately 400 hymns and adapted several others during his lifetime. His poem titled "Nativity" has stood the test of time. Initially published in the *Sheffield Iris* on December 24, 1816, it eventually became the song "Angels from the Realms of Glory."

Music - Henry Smart (1813-1879)

Henry Smart was a mostly self-taught musician and a designer and builder of organs who served as organist for various churches in London. Despite being almost blind for the last 15 years of his life, he continued to play and write music and created unrivaled standards of congregational singing.

Smart edited the *Presbyterian Psalms and Hymns for Divine Worship* in 1866. This publication includes one of his tunes, "Regent Square," the tune that is used for "Angels from the Realms of Glory" in America.

In the UK, the French tune known as "Iris" is used for "Angels from the Realms of Glory." "Iris" is associated with the French carol, "Les Anges dans nos Campagnes." Americans use the "Iris" tune for "Angels We Have Heard on High." Given the similarities between the opening lines of the two songs, it's perhaps not surprising that they are sometimes sung to the same tune.

Sources

Bradley, Ian (ed.) *The Penguin Book of Carols.* Penguin Books, 1999, pp. 27-29.

Collins, Ace. *Stories Behind the Best-Loved Songs of Christmas.* Zondervan, 2001, pp. 11-17.

Gant, Andrew. *Carols of Christmas: A Celebration of the Surprising Stories Behind Your Favorite Holiday Songs,* Thomas Nelson, 2015, pp. 239-240.

Keyte, Hugh and Parrott, Andrew, editors. *The New Oxford Book of Carols.* Oxford University Press, 1998, p. 351.

Mosteller, Angie. *Christmas Songs Stories Behind the Classic Songs of Christmas,* 2010, pp. 8-9.

Les Anges Dans Nos Campagnes

1. Les anges dans nos campagnes
   Ont entonné l'hymne des cieux,
   Et l'écho de nos montagnes
   Redit ce chant mélodieux:

   Gloria in excelsis Deo,
   Gloria in excelsis Deo.

2. Bergers, pour qui cette fête?
   Quel est l'objet de tous ces chants?
   Quel vainqueur, quelle conquête
   Mérite ces cris triomphants?
   Gloria in excelsis Deo,
   Gloria in excelsis Deo.

3. Ils annoncent la naissance
   Du libérateur d'Israël,
   Et, pleins de reconnaissance
   Chantent en ce jour solennel:
   Gloria in excelsis Deo,
   Gloria in excelsis Deo.

Source: https://hymnary.org/hymn/CBOW1994/321 (Catholic Book of Worship) Accessed August 28, 2024.

Angels from the Realms of Glory

1. Angels from the realms of glory,
   Wing your flight o'er all the earth;
   Ye who sang creation's story
   Now proclaim Messiah's birth:

   Refrain:
   Come and worship, come and worship,
   Worship Christ, the newborn King.

2. Shepherds, in the field abiding,
   Watching o'er your flocks by night,
   God with us is now residing;
   Yonder shines the infant light:

3. Sages, leave your contemplations,
   Brighter visions beam afar;
   Seek the great Desire of nations;
   Ye have seen His natal star:

4. Saints, before the altar bending,
   Watching long in hope and fear;
   Suddenly the Lord, descending,
   In His temple shall appear:

5. Sinners, wrung with true repentance,
   Doomed for guilt to endless pains,
   Justice now revokes the sentence,
   Mercy calls you; break your chains:

6. Though an Infant now we view Him,
   He shall fill His Father's throne,
   Gather all the nations to Him;
   Every knee shall then bow down:

7. All creation, join in praising
   God, the Father, Spirit, Son,
   Evermore your voices raising
   To th'eternal Three in One:

Joy to the World

"Joy to the World," was written by Isaac Watts, who, in addition to being one of England's best-known preachers, was also an educator and author. He wrote books on astronomy and philosophy that were used in universities but is best remembered for his hymns.

Words - Isaac Watts (1674 – 1748)

Isaac Watts was born in 1674, in Southampton, England, while his father was in prison for going against the teachings of both the Church of England and the scholars of his time. He was very intelligent and learned French, Greek, Latin and Hebrew by the age of thirteen. He may have attended Cambridge or Oxford for his education if he had been a member of the Church of England, but instead, he was sent to the Independent Academy (otherwise known as the Dissenters' Academy) at Stoke Newington.

Watts attended Above Bar Congregational Church and found church music to be rather boring. He didn't sense any joy in the songs that were sung in services and complained to his father, who challenged him to come up with better alternatives. Isaac took up this challenge and his first song was met with enthusiasm by his father's church. In fact, they asked for a new hymn each week, and Isaac wrote several hymns over the next two years, after which he moved to London. There, he joined the Mark Lane Independent Church and became the Senior Pastor in 1702, a position which he would hold for the rest of his life.

An unintended Christmas song

Watts set out to paraphrase most of the 150 Psalms and compiled "The Psalms of David Imitated in the Language of the New Testament and Applied to the Christian State and Worship." The lyrics of "Joy to the World" were inspired by Psalm 98, specifically verses 4-9. The project was published in 1719 and garnered mixed reactions. Despite the popularity of the hymns, some people opposed their use in church services. Some even went as far as referring to Watts as an agent of the devil. At the time, people were used to singing metrical psalms, and they believed that singing anything other than words from the Bible would be offensive to God.

In America, Benjamin Franklin published Watt's hymns in 1729, and the controversies continued. Forty years after Watts' death, someone reportedly petitioned the General Assembly of the Presbyterian Church in Philadelphia to refuse the use of Watts' hymns in public worship.

A prolific hymn writer

Over the course of his lifetime, Isaac Watts composed over six hundred hymns and poems. The famous hymn "When I Survey the Wondrous Cross" was published in *Hymns and Spiritual Songs,* in 1707, as part of Watts' second collection of hymns, the first having been published the previous year. Another well-known hymn that was composed by Isaac Watts is "We're Marching to Zion." In 1715, Watts published *Divine Songs for the Use of Children,* a collection of songs for children. Watts died on November 25, 1748, in Stoke Newington, London.

Music - Lowell Mason (1792 – 1872)

Lowell Mason was born in 1792, forty-four years after Isaac Newton's death. Although he was musically gifted, he didn't think he could make a living as a musician and pursued a career in banking. He wrote musical melodies and studied the music of the German composer, Handel. His first attempt to get his musical arrangements published was met with rejection. The publisher felt that Americans would not be interested in classical music but would rather prefer new folk music. After this initial disappointment, Mason continued playing the organ in a local church. Eventually, the Handel and Hayden Society of Massachusetts offered to publish the work in 1822, even though Mason requested that his name be omitted from the title page. He was still working as a banker and didn't want to be known as a musician. It was only after thousands of copies of his work had been sold and used by schools and church choirs that he decided to devote his efforts to music.

Antioch

In 1836, Mason published Isaac Watts' Psalm 98-inspired poem together with a tune he attributed to George Handel in a booklet titled *Occasional Psalm and Hymn Tunes*. The tune is believed to have been inspired by Handel's Messiah and was originally titled "Antioch."

The work of two "fathers" combined

Isaac Watts was known as the "father of English Hymnody" and Lowell Mason was known as the "father of American church music." How appropriate that, together they would produce this most beloved Christmas carol announcing the birth of Christ!

How "Joy to the World" became associated with Christmas remains a mystery. It was inspired by a passage from the Old Testament, and except for the phrase "The Lord is Come," doesn't make any reference to the birth of Christ. Regardless, it is a Christmas favorite, worthy of being sung all year round.

Sources

Mosteller, Angie. Christmas Songs - Stories Behind the Classic Songs of Christmas, 2010, pp. 54-58.

Bradley, Ian (ed.) *The Penguin Book of Carols*, Penguin Books, 1999, pp. 177-180.

Collins, Ace. *Stories Behind the Best-Loved Songs of Christmas*, Zondervan, 2001, pp. 107-113.

Joy to the World

1. Joy to the World, the Lord is come!
   Let earth receive her King
   Let every heart prepare Him room
   And Heaven and nature sing
   And Heaven and nature sing
   And Heaven, and Heaven, and nature sing

2. Joy to the World, the Savior reigns!
   Let men their songs employ
   While fields and floods, rocks, hills and plains
   Repeat the sounding joy
   Repeat the sounding joy
   Repeat, repeat, the sounding joy

3. No more let sins and sorrows grow
   Nor thorns infest the ground
   He comes to make His blessings flow
   Far as the curse is found
   Far as the curse is found
   Far as, far as, the curse is found

4. He rules the world with truth and grace
   And makes the nations prove
   The glories of His righteousness
   And wonders of His love
   And wonders of His love
   And wonders, wonders, of His love

Psalm 98:4-9 (King James Version)

4Make a joyful noise unto the LORD, all the earth: make a loud noise, and rejoice, and sing praise.

5Sing unto the LORD with the harp; with the harp, and the voice of a psalm.

6With trumpets and sound of cornet make a joyful noise before the LORD, the King.

7Let the sea roar, and the fulness thereof; the world, and they that dwell therein.

8Let the floods clap *their* hands: let the hills be joyful together

9Before the LORD; for he cometh to judge the earth: with righteousness shall he judge the world, and the people with equity.

Angels We Have Heard on High

Words – Anonymous

"Angels We Have Heard on High" is believed to have originated in France, and the earliest known version is from a French book that was published in the 1800s. (1819, 1842 and 1855 have been cited as publication dates, depending on the source). This song can be described as macaronic, due to the inclusion of words from more than one language. The use of Latin suggests that it was written by a Catholic monk or priest.

Translator - James Chadwick (1813-1882)

"Les Anges dans nos Campagnes" was translated into English ("Angels We Have Heard on High") in 1840 by a Roman Catholic bishop, James Chadwick. He was born in Ireland to an Irish mother and English father. Chadwick was dedicated to prayer and meditation, and this is reflected in his publications, which included: *Instructions How to Meditate* and *St. Theresa's own words: Instructions on the Prayer of Recollection*.

Music - Arranged by Edward Shippen Barnes (1887-1958)

The origin of the melody of this song is also unknown, but its simplicity suggests a possible link to chants used by monks. The notes are restricted to an octave, the verse only includes six notes and there is little variation in the chorus. Even though the word "Gloria" is spread over three measures and includes almost twenty notes, this song is still relatively easy to sing, when compared with many other carols.

The version of the tune commonly used, "Gloria" (also known as "Iris"), was arranged by Edward Shippen Barnes, a Yale University-trained organist, who also studied at the Schola Cantorum in Paris, France. Barnes composed organ symphonies and wrote an instructional book for organ players but is best remembered for his musical arrangement of "Angels We Have Heard on High." In the U.K., this tune is used for "Angels from the Realms of Glory."

Sources

Collins, Ace. *Stories Behind the Best-Loved Songs of Christmas*. Zondervan, 2001, pp. 18-23.

Mosteller, Angie. *Christmas Songs Stories Behind the Classic Songs of Christmas*, 2010, pp. 12-13.

Angels We Have Heard on High

1. Angels we have heard on high
   Sweetly singing o'er the plains
   And the mountains in reply
   Echoing their joyous strains

   Gloria, in excelsis Deo!
   Gloria, in excelsis Deo!

2. Shepherds, why this jubilee?
   Why your joyous strains prolong?
   What the gladsome tidings be
   Which inspire your heavenly song?

   Gloria, in excelsis Deo!
   Gloria, in excelsis Deo!

3   Come to Bethlehem and see
    Him Whose birth the angels sing;
    Come, adore on bended knee,
    Christ the Lord, the newborn King.

    Gloria, in excelsis Deo!
    Gloria, in excelsis Deo!

4. See Him in a manger laid
    Jesus Lord of heaven and earth;
    Mary, Joseph, lend your aid,
    With us sing our Savior's birth.
    Gloria, in excelsis Deo!
    Gloria, in excelsis Deo!

O Holy Night

A legendary carol

According to legend, "O Holy Night" was sung during the Franco-Prussian War of 1871 and fighting ceased temporarily while the French troops sang it to their opponents on Christmas Eve. As fascinating as the story sounds, it is not verifiable. Despite this, it has become such an integral part of the history of "O Holy Night" and continues to be repeated, often without question.

Regardless of whether this story is true or not, "O Holy Night" has had a profound impact on so many people around the world. The December 2020 issue of americamagazine.org features a lesser-known story that demonstrates the nurturing power of this song, particularly in wartime. According to the article, The Rev. Ron Camarda, a Catholic priest and Marine Reserve major, sang "O Holy Night" at the bedside of a dying American Marine in Fallujah, Iraq, to convey a message of love from home.

A French Poem

"O Holy Night" has its origin in a French poem, "Minuit, Chretiens" (Midnight, Christians) by Placide Cappeau. He was an unlikely choice since he wasn't particularly religious. Some writers even describe him as an atheist. The poem was set to music by Adolphe Charles Adams, and it became very popular in France.

"Cantique de Noel," as the song was originally known, is said to have been banned from church services in France, despite its popularity. The church leaders felt it was unfit for church services due to what they felt was a lack of musical taste and the absence of religious spirit. Some sources also attribute the ban to the identities of the composers, Placide Cappeau being a socialist and Adolphe Adam supposedly Jewish. However, according to the New World Encyclopedia, there is no evidence for the claim that Adam was Jewish. It was also documented that he had a Catholic burial. After the song was rejected in France, it was introduced to America through John Sullivan Dwight, a Unitarian minister.

First song on live radio?

"O Holy Night" is said to have been the first song that was broadcast live on radio. Reginald Fessenden was a Canadian inventor and a protégé of Thomas Edison. As the story goes, Fessenden said that on December 21, 1906, he played "O Holy Night" on the violin, after reading a passage from the gospel of Luke.

Some historians have questioned this claim and James E. O'Neal reviews the lack of supporting documentation in an essay titled: Fessenden – World's First Broadcaster?

According to the website earlyradiohistory.us, Fessenden developed an alternator-transmitter in late 1906, and though the possibility of using it for music and information was noted at the time, his subsequent work focused on developing it as an adjunct to the telephone system, as opposed to broadcasting.

The website also includes the following excerpt from one of Fessenden's letters:

"The program on Christmas Eve was as follows: first a short speech by me saying what we were going to do, then some phonograph music. --The music on the phonograph being Handel's 'Largo'. Then came a violin solo by me, being a composition of Gounod called 'O, Holy Night', and ending up with the words 'Adore and be still' of which I sang one verse, in addition to playing on the violin, though the singing of course was not very good. Then came the Bible text, 'Glory to God in the highest and on earth peace to men of good will', and finally we wound up by wishing them a Merry Christmas and then saying that we proposed to broadcast again New Year's Eve….."

A detailed discussion regarding the veracity of the claim that Fessenden was the first to transmit an entertainment broadcast over the radio is beyond the scope of this book, but the reference to "O, Holy Night" quoted above is significant. The letter refers to the song as a composition of Gounod, which it is not. "Adore and be still," is actually the title of one of Gounod's compositions,

though in the letter Fessenden writes that those are the words that the song ("O Holy Night") concludes with. There appears to be enough evidence to seriously question the claim that "O Holy Night" was the first song to be broadcast on the radio. One explanation that has been given is that Fessenden suffered a memory lapse in his telling of the story. This seems likely, based on his writing quoted above. Unfortunately, this part of the "O Holy Night" story has been repeated so many times that it, too, like the Christmas Eve 1871 story, is generally accepted as fact.

Creators of the Carol

Words - Placide Cappeau (1808-1877)

Placide Cappeau was born in Roquemaure, France to Mathieu Cappeau and Agathe Louise Martinet.

Unfortunately, he lost his hand as a result of a shooting accident at the age of eight when a friend accidentally shot him. The friend's father paid for part of his education, and he studied at the Royal College of Avignon, winning an award for drawing in 1825. Cappeau earned degrees in literature and law, eventually returning to his hometown, where he joined the mayor in the wine trade. While pursuing a career as a wine merchant, Cappeau wrote poetry in his spare time. In 1843, Father Joseph Marie Gilles, the local priest, asked him to write a Christmas song to celebrate the restoration of the church organ. Despite being "anti-cleric," Cappeau agreed and wrote the lyrics based on verses in the book of Luke. A local singer, Mrs. Laurey, heard about the poem and asked her friend Adolphe Adam to compose the music for it, with the intent of singing it at the Christmas service that year (1843). Unfortunately, that goal was not achieved, as she went to Paris and didn't return for several years. Her wish was finally fulfilled during the Christmas season of 1847 when she returned to Roquemaure. Unfortunately, Father Gilles, at whose request the original poem had been written, died in 1846, without hearing the version that was set to music.

Music - Adolphe Charles Adam (1803-1856)

Adolphe Adam was born in Paris in 1803. His father was a well-known classical musician, and his mother was the daughter of a physician. Adolphe's father, Louis was initially opposed to the idea of his son following in his footsteps, but Adolphe secretly took music lessons from an older friend. Louis later allowed Adolphe to study at the Conservatoire but insisted that he should not make a career out of music. Adolphe entered the Paris Conservatoire in 1817 but had a nonchalant attitude towards the formal study of music. Fortunately, a teacher named Boieldieu took an interest in him, helped to nurture his talent, and even encouraged him to write music. He eventually became very prolific, composing operas, ballets and full orchestra pieces.

Adolphe Adam went on to win the second prize in the Prix de Rome competition in 1825, having received an honorable mention the year before. He is perhaps best known for his 1841 ballet Giselle, ou les Wilis.

By 1847, he was successful enough to open his own opera house. Unfortunately, due to the political unrest of that period, the opera house closed only four months after opening, and Adam lost his investments and capital.

Due to his popularity and the success of his new compositions, he was able to pay off his debt while supporting himself as a musical journalist. He became a composition professor at the Conservatoire in 1849 and by 1852, his debt was paid off. Unfortunately, Adam did not live to witness the phenomenal success that became of the carol he helped create. He died in 1856, at the age of 52. There is no mention of "O Holy Night" in Adam's posthumously published memoirs, suggesting that he didn't attach much importance to the song.

Translator - John Sullivan Dwight (1813-1893)

John Sullivan Dwight was the great-grandson of the famous American revivalist preacher Jonathan Edwards. His father, Timothy Dwight, served as president of Yale University and chaplain to George Washington during the Revolutionary War. Timothy Dwight made his mark in the world of church music when he published Isaac Watts' psalms in 1801.

John Dwight attended Harvard College and Divinity School and became a Unitarian minister. He reportedly was unable to continue in the ministry due to experiencing panic attacks when he had to face the congregation. At times he would lock himself at home, scared to go out in public. He eventually became a

classical music critic and a musical editor for various magazines. He founded an influential musical publication, *Dwight's Journal of Music* in 1852. It was while searching for songs for this journal that he found "Minuit, Chretiens," which he translated to "O Holy Night." An abolitionist, he modified the lyrics to include the reference to breaking the chains of slavery. The English version was published in Dwight's magazine and other songbooks and was especially popular in the North during the Civil War.

A Carol for All Times

Some people thought "O Holy Night" was too much like an opera, while others thought it was too 'war-like,' with Adolphe Adam even referring to it as the 'the religious Marseillaise.' Regardless of the fuzziness of some of the details and the associated controversies, the story of this beloved carol is fascinating and inspiring. Almost two centuries after it was first written, it continues to inspire people and has been recorded by several contemporary musicians, including Celine Dion, Nat King Cole, Mariah Carey and Josh Groban.

Sources

Collins, Ace. *Stories Behind the Best-Loved Songs of Christmas.* Zondervan, 2001, pp. 132-138.

Gant, Andrew. *Carols of Christmas: A Celebration of the Surprising Stories Behind Your Favorite Holiday Songs.* Thomas Nelson, 2015, pp. 203-204.

Mosteller, Angie. Christmas Songs Stories Behind the Classic Songs of Christmas, 2010, pp. 78-83.

A brief history of 'O Holy Night,' the rousing Christmas hymn that garnered mixed reviews | America Magazine. Accessed 6/11/2024.

How "O Holy Night" became a popular Christmas carol (galaxymusicnotes.com). Accessed June 11, 2024.

https://www.allmusic.com/artist/adolphe-adam-mn0000394866. Accessed August 7, 2024.

https://earlyradiohistory.us/1940fes2.htm. Accessed August 7, 2024.

https://www.frenchlearner.com/songs/minuit-chretien-o-holy-night-french-lyrics/. Accessed August 27, 2024.

http://www.musimem.com/minuit-chretiens.htm. Accessed August 7, 2024.

https://www.newworldencyclopedia.org/entry/Adolphe_Adam. Accessed June 11, 2024.

http://www.radioworld.com/headlines/0045/fessenden-worlds-first-broadcaster/311783. Accessed August 7, 2024.

https://www.umc.org/en/content/the-intriguing-history-of-o-holy-night. Accessed June 11, 2024.

O Holy Night

1. O holy night, the stars are brightly shining,
   It is the night of the dear Savior's birth;
   Long lay the world in sin and error pining,
   'Till he appeared and the soul felt its worth.
   A thrill of hope the weary world rejoices,
   For yonder breaks a new and glorious morn;

   Chorus
   Fall on your knees, Oh hear the angel voices!
   O night divine! O night when Christ was born.
   O night, O holy night, O night divine.

2. Led by the light of Faith serenely beaming;
   With glowing hearts by his cradle we stand:
   So, led by light of a star sweetly gleaming,
   Here come the wise men from Orient land,
   The King of Kings lay thus in lowly manger,
   In all our trials born to be our friend;

   Chorus
   He knows our need, To our weakness no stranger!
   Behold your King! Before Him lowly bend!
   Behold your King! your King! before him bend!

3. Truly He taught us to love one another;
   His law is Love and His gospel is Peace;
   Chains shall he break, for the slave is our brother,
   And in his name all oppression shall cease,
   Sweet hymns of joy in grateful Chorus raise we;
   Let all within us praise his Holy name!

   Chorus
   Christ is the Lord, then ever! ever praise we!
   His pow'r and glory, evermore proclaim!
   His pow'r and glory, evermore proclaim!

Minuit! Chrétiens

Minuit! Chrétiens, c'est l'heure solennelle
Où l'homme Dieu descendit jusqu'à nous,
Pour effacer la tache originelle
Et de son père arrêter le courroux:
Le monde entier tressaille d'espérance
A cette nuit qui lui donne un sauveur
Peuple à genoux, attends ta délivrance
Noël ! Noël ! Voici le Rédempteur !
Noël ! Noël ! Voici le Rédempteur !

De notre foi que la lumière ardente
Nous guide tous au berceau de l'enfant
Comme autrefois, une étoile brillante
Y conduisit les chefs de l'Orient
Le Roi des Rois naît dans une humble crèche,
Puissants du jour fiers de votre grandeur,
A votre orgueil c'est de là qu'un Dieu prêche,
Courbez vos fronts devant le Rédempteur !
Courbez vos fronts devant le Rédempteur !

Source:

https://www.frenchlearner.com/songs/minuit-chretien-o-holy-night-french-lyrics/

Accessed August 27, 2024.

Midnight! Christians

Midnight! Christians, it's the solemn hour
When the man God came down to us,
To wipe away the original sin
And stop the wrath of His Father
The entire world jumped for joy with hope
To this night that gives Him a Savior
People on their knees, awaiting your deliverance
Christmas! Christmas! Here's the Redeemer!
Christmas! Christmas! Here's the Redeemer!

It's from our faith that the blazing light
Guides all of us to the cradle of the child
Like in the past, a bright star
And drive the leaders from the East
The King of kings was born in a humble manger
Powerful of proud days of Your greatness
To your pride, it's from from there that God preaches
Bow your heads in before the Redeemer!
Bow your heads in before the Redeemer!

Mary's Boy Child

"Mary's Boy Child" was written by Jester Hairston, a Julliard-trained songwriter. He composed a song for a birthday party at a friend's request and titled the song "He Pone and Chocolate Tea." When he was later asked to compose a Christmas song for a choir, he came up with new lyrics for the tune he had composed earlier, and "Mary's Boy Child" was born.

Composer - Jester Hairston (1901-2000)

The grandson of slaves, Hairston was born in Belews Creek, North Carolina. He lost his father to an accident as a young boy and was raised by his grandmother while his mother worked. He grew up listening to his grandmother and her friends talk and sing about plantation life and was determined to preserve history through music. Hairston composed or arranged over 300 choral spirituals. He also composed film scores, including "Amen," a song dubbed for Sidney Poitier in the film "Lilies of the Field." Hairston received a star on the Hollywood Walk of Fame for his contributions to film and television.

Famous recording - Harry Belafonte (1927-2023)

Harry Belafonte heard "Mary's Boy Child" performed by Schumann's Hollywood Choir and asked for permission to record it, which he did, releasing a single in 1956. The next year, it was released by RCA Victor (Sony Music) as part of the album "An Evening with Belafonte," and became a bestselling record.

"Mary's Boy Child" was also released in the UK as a single, reaching number one on the singles chart in November 1957, and selling over a million copies there. There are various versions of the song, including a version by Boney M., who returned the song to the top of the British charts in 1978, with Mary's Boy Child/Oh My Lord.

Harry Belafonte was born in New York in 1927 and spent some of his early years in Jamaica. He popularized calypso music, and some of his best-known songs include "Banana Boat Song" and "Jamaica Farewell."

In addition, to being a singer, Belafonte was an actor and civil rights activist.

Breaking racial barriers

Both Hairston and Belafonte were known for breaking racial barriers. Hairston was the first African American to be invited to conduct the Mormon Tabernacle Choir. He was also active in organizing Hairston family reunions and sponsored reunions for both Black and White descendants. Belafonte was the first Black

male to have a number-one hit in the UK and his record was the first to sell a million copies in the UK. Harry Belafonte died in 2023 at the age of 96.

Dr. Charles Steele, Jr., president and CEO of the Southern Christian Leadership Conference, made the statements below, reflecting on Belafonte's life and legacy.

"He always told me to hang in there and to never give up. He inspired me many years before we met… …. One of my favorite quotes by Mr. Belafonte was his recollection of a private moment with Dr. King, who was discouraged about America's inability to address the nation's growing poverty after some civil rights successes regarding integration. He said 'Harry, I think I have integrated my people into a burning house. I forgot about the economics.' Mr. Belafonte understood that it takes money to enjoy the basics of what America has to offer. Unfortunately, we are still in that burning house. Thank you, Mr. Belafonte, for leading the way in the spirit of Dr. King as well as for yourself. Your contributions will be a part of our movement forever."

The full statement can be found at this site https://nationalsclc.org/sclc-bids-farewell-to-harry-belafonte/.

Both Hairston and Belafonte demonstrated that music can have an impact far beyond its entertainment value. Music can be used as a bridge builder, connecting and uniting people who may otherwise have little in common. It can also be used to advocate for equal rights and justice.

Sources

Bradley, Ian (ed.) *The Penguin Book of Carols*, Penguin Books, 1999, p. 192.

https://www.songfacts.com/facts/harry-belafonte/marys-boy-child. Accessed June 26, 2024.

https://nationalsclc.org/sclc-bids-farewell-to-harry-belafonte/. Accessed August 16, 2024.

https://thedeaconsbench.com/the-composer-behind-marys-boy-child/. Accessed August 1, 2024.

O Come, O Come, Emmanuel

O Come, O Come, Emmanuel could very well be the oldest Christmas carol around. Its author is unknown, but it is believed to have been written by a monk or priest prior to 800 AD.

This song originated from the "Great Antiphons," or "Great O's," part of the medieval Roman Catholic Advent liturgy, and was originally written in Latin. Antiphon means "opposite voice," and refers to a responsive form of chant or song. The seven great antiphons are believed to date from the eighth century. They were sung or chanted on the seven evenings preceding Christmas Eve, in anticipation of Christ's birth. Each one refers to a Messianic title.

- O **S**apentia (Wisdom)
- O **A**donai (God)
- O **R**adix Jesse (Stem or root of Jesse)
- O **C**lavis David (Key of David)
- O **O**riens (Dayspring)
- O **R**ex genitium (King of the Gentiles)
- O **E**mmanuel (God with us)

Translator - John Mason Neale (1818 – 1866)

John Mason Neale, an Anglican priest, scholar and hymn writer, was born on January 24, 1818. He was educated at Trinity College in Cambridge and spoke more than twenty languages. His intelligence and insight appear to have been threatening to those around him, as he was sent off to the Madeira Islands off the Northwest coast of Africa to avoid spreading his "radical" ideas in England. While there, he established the Sisterhood of St. Margaret, an orphanage, a school for girls and a house of refuge for prostitutes.

In the early 1800s, some theologians from Oxford University were concerned about the decline of the Anglican church. They felt that the quality of worship and liturgy had been secularized and wanted to revitalize the church. The Oxford Movement, the name by which they came to be known, took steps to elevate the quality of church music, in addition to restoring traditional liturgy. John Mason Neale was very influential in the work of improving the hymns sung in the Anglican Church. He researched hymns, including Latin hymns, with the intent of translating them and introducing them to the church.

During his research, Neale came across a 1610 publication titled *Psalteroium Cantionum Catholicarum,* which contained the words of the Latin chant, "Veni, Veni, Emmanuel." He translated the text to English, resulting in a version that started with the words "Draw nigh, draw nigh, Emmanuel." The song was later shortened from seven to five verses and titled "O Come, O Come, Emmanuel." It was published in *Hymns Ancient and Modern* in 1861.

Music - Thomas Helmore (1811-1890)

Thomas Helmore wanted to restore congregational singing, but he disapproved of the style of hymns used in the Church of England. He was a friend of John Mason Neale's, and he played a major role in reviving ancient chant melodies. Helmore paired the tune "Veni, Veni Emmanuel" with the English translation and published it in the *Hymnal Noted* in 1851. The original composer of the tune "Veni, Veni Emmanuel" is unknown, but it is believed to have originated in a 15th-century French processional melody that was used during funerals. Helmore's disapproval of the style of hymns used in the Church of England at the time suggests that he probably didn't anticipate that "O Come, O Come Emmanuel" would end up being published alongside the works of famous hymn writers like Isaac Watts.

Sources

Mosteller, Angie. *Christmas Songs - Stories behind the classic songs of Christmas*, 2010, pp. 73-76.

Collins, Ace. *Stories Behind the Best-Loved Songs of Christmas*, Zondervan, 2001, pp. 126-131.

Gant, Andrew. *Carols of Christmas: A Celebration of the Surprising Stories Behind Your Favorite Holiday Songs*, Thomas Nelson, 2015, pp. 45-46.

https://www.stjohnfredonia.org/post/o-come-o-come-emmanuel-a-brief-history. Accessed July 31, 2024.

O Come, O Come, Emmanuel

1. O come, O come, Emmanuel
   And ransom captive Israel
   That mourns in lonely exile here
   Until the Son of God appear
   Rejoice! Rejoice! Emmanuel
   Shall come to thee, O Israel.

2. O come, Thou Rod of Jesse, free
   Thine own from Satan's tyranny
   From depths of hell Thy people save
   And give them victory o'er the grave
   Rejoice! Rejoice! Emmanuel
   Shall come to thee, O Israel.

3. O come, Thou Day-Spring, come and cheer
   Our spirits by Thine advent here
   Disperse the gloomy clouds of night
   And death's dark shadows put to flight.
   Rejoice! Rejoice! Emmanuel
   Shall come to thee, O Israel.

4. O come, Thou Key of David, come,
   And open wide our heavenly home;
   Make safe the way that leads on high,
   And close the path to misery.
   Rejoice! Rejoice! Emmanuel
   Shall come to thee, O Israel.

5. O come, O come, Thou Lord of might,
   Who to Thy tribes, on Sinai's height,
   In ancient times did'st give the Law,
   In cloud, and majesty and awe.
   Rejoice! Rejoice! Emmanuel
   Shall come to thee, O Israel.

It Came Upon the Midnight Clear

"It Came Upon the Midnight Clear" is one of the first Christmas carols that was produced by Americans.

Words - Edmund Sears (1810-1876)

"It Came Upon the Midnight Clear" was written by Edmund Sears in 1849. He was born in Berkshire County, Massachusetts, and had a love for poetry as a child. He authored his first Christmas poem at age 24 while attending the Harvard Divinity School. He graduated in 1837 and wrote several religious books.

Sears was disturbed by slavery and poverty and belonged to the Unitarian Church, which prioritized social justice. He believed that Christians should reach out to the helpless and poor, and wanted to inspire his congregation with an uplifting Christmas message but was having trouble lifting up his own spirit. Upset by the poverty and hopelessness around him, he searched for the right words, and was touched by this passage from the book of Luke:

And there were shepherds living out in the fields nearby, keeping watch over their flocks at night. An angel of the Lord appeared to them, and the glory of the Lord shone around them, and they were terrified.
- Luke 2:8-9 (NIV)

These words inspired Sears to write the poem "It Came Upon the Midnight Clear."

He retrieved another poem he had written a decade earlier, titled "Calm on the Listening Ear of Night Comes Heaven's Melodious Strains." He then wrote a Christmas message that started with the older poem and ended with the new one.

In addition to being a preacher, Sears was also editor of a newspaper and a magazine, which gave him access to a wider audience. "It Came Upon the Midnight Clear" was published in *The Christian Register* in its December 29, 1849 issue, and later in *Sermons and Songs of the Christian Life*.

Sears was forced into early retirement in the 1850s due to poor health. He focused on writing for the rest of his life and died in 1876.

Music - Richard Storrs Willis (1819-1900)

The tune used for "It Came Upon the Midnight Clear" in America was originally composed for the organ by Richard Storrs Willis, and subsequently rearranged as a hymn by Uzziah Christopher Burnap. Richard Storrs Willis had been composing choral music from an early age and graduated from Yale

University in 1841. He studied with prominent musicians in Germany, learned German and returned to Yale to teach the language. He also became the music critic for the *New York Tribune* and published several collections of music.

Different tunes, same song

In Britain, this song has been associated with different tunes, most commonly "Noel," a traditional carol that was rearranged by Arthur Sullivan. In America, Willis discovered Sears' poem and saw that one of his tunes, "Carol," fit perfectly with the text. He published the text and music in 1850, with the title "Study No. 23" and published a new arrangement a decade later.

Inspiration in time of war

Like many other Christmas carols, this song of hope and peace has been an inspiration, particularly in times of war. American soldiers sang it throughout France during World War I and at the frontlines during World War II.

Sources

Bradley, Ian (ed.) *The Penguin Book of Carols*, Penguin Books, 1999, pp. 160-163.

Collins, Ace. *Stories Behind the Best-Loved Songs of Christmas*, Zondervan, 2001, pp. 96-101.

Mosteller, Angie. *Christmas Songs- Stories behind the classic songs of Christmas*, 2010, pp. 49-51.

Calm On the Listening Ear of Night | Hymnary.org. Accessed August 28, 2024.

It Came Upon the Midnight Clear

1. It came upon a midnight clear,
   That glorious song of old,
   From angels bending near the earth,
   To touch their harps of gold:
   "Peace on the earth, goodwill to men,
   From heaven's all-gracious King."
   The world in solemn stillness lay,
   To hear the angels sing.

2. Still through the cloven skies they come,
   With peaceful wings unfurled,
   And still their heavenly music floats
   O'er all the weary world;
   Above its sad and lowly plains,
   They bend on hovering wing,
   And ever o'er its Babel sounds
   The blessèd angels sing.

3. Yet with the woes of sin and strife
   The world has suffered long;
   Beneath the angel-strain have rolled
   Two thousand years of wrong;
   And man, at war with man, hears not
   The love-song which they bring;
   O hush the noise, ye men of strife,
   And hear the angels sing.

4. And ye, beneath life's crushing load,
   Whose forms are bending low,
   Who toil along the climbing way
   With painful steps and slow,
   Look now! for glad and golden hours
   come swiftly on the wing.
   O rest beside the weary road,
   And hear the angels sing!

5. For lo!, the days are hastening on,
   By prophet bards foretold,
   When with the ever-circling years
   Comes round the age of gold
   When peace shall over all the earth
   Its ancient splendors fling,
   And the whole world give back the song
   Which now the angels sing.

Silver Bells

"Silver Bells" was written in 1950 and sung by Bob Hope and Marilyn Maxwell in the movie *The Lemon Drop Kid*. Bob Hope had been scheduled for a remake of the movie, in which he played the role of a gambler who was unable to pay off the large sum of money he owed. His character was to sing a song or two in the film.

Words and music

Ray Evans (1915-2007) and Jay Livingston (1915-2001)

Ray Evans and Jay Livingston were amateur musicians and had played together in a college orchestra, *The Continentals,* while attending the University of Pennsylvania. The orchestra played on cruise ships during vacations. They became friends and bought Cuban instruments in Havana, which they played on the ship. As the story goes, the cruise director liked their music and offered them the opportunity to play on future cruises. After their last cruise, they stayed in New York and became songwriters, with Ray writing the lyrics and Jay composing the music. They worked for Paramount Studios for ten years, starting from 1945, and won two Oscars during that time.

When Evans and Livingston were asked to write the score for a film, they were skeptical about writing yet another Christmas song, with so many already in existence. Noting that most other Christmas films were set in the country, they decided to come up with a song that had a different theme. While they were brainstorming, one of them picked up a small silver bell and started playing with it.

The duo began to think about the decorations in the streets and display windows of New York, anxious shoppers, children's faces and the Salvation Army bell ringers outside the stores. They wrote a song and decided to share it with Jay's wife before sharing it with Bob Hope.

To their surprise, she started laughing at their new song! She told them that the chorus wouldn't work and that others would laugh when they heard it, too.

As originally written, the chorus was:

"Tinker bell, tinker bell, it's Christmastime in the city"

The men listened to the song again and decided to change the word "tinker" to "silver," and "Silver Bells" was born!

A song about the Christmas scene in the city was timely, as many Americans had moved into urban areas after World War II and were experiencing Christmas in the city. The reference to the traffic lights "blinking red and green" tells us something about the history of the traffic lights – the orange caution light hadn't yet been added at the time.

Famous recording - Bing Crosby (1903-1977)

The first recording of "Silver Bells" was released by Decca Records in 1950. It featured Bing Crosby and Carol Richards with John Scott Trotter and His Orchestra and the Lee Gordon Singers. The movie *The Lemon Drop Kid* was not released till the next year. The song was performed by Bob Hope and Marilyn Maxwell in the movie. "Silver Bells" has been recorded by several other artists, including Loretta Lynn (1966) and Stevie Wonder (1967).

After *The Lemon Drop Kid* movie was released, Bob Hope continued to sing "Silver Bells" to US troops at Christmas for more than forty years. "Silver Bells" was played in the White House, with then President John F. Kennedy declaring it his favorite Christmas carol.

Sources

Collins, Ace. *Stories Behind the Best-Loved Songs of Christmas*, Zondervan, 2001, pp. 159-163.

https://blogs.loc.gov/nls-music-notes/2022/12/silver-bells/. Accessed August 15, 2024.

I'll Be Home for Christmas

"I'll Be Home for Christmas" is another favorite that has brought hope and inspiration to many people. It was first released in 1943, during World War II, when the separation of families caused by the war made the longing to be together for the holidays particularly intense.

It may come as a surprise to most people that this song was the result of a collaboration between a lawyer and an architect.

Words - James Kimball "Kim" Gannon (1900-1974)

James "Kim" Gannon wrote the words for "I'll Be Home for Christmas." He was an American songwriter and composer, and he attended St. Lawrence University, where he met his wife and wrote the school's alma mater. He graduated from St. Lawrence University in 1924 and later attended Albany Law School, graduating from the latter in 1934. While at law school, he worked as a radio broadcaster under the pseudonym Johnny Albright.

According to the Albany Law School website, a quote from his yearbook reads:

"Give Kim time and he will have all the law set to music." ★

Music - Walter Kent (1911-1994)

Walter Kent, an American composer and songwriter, composed the music for "I'll Be Home for Christmas." Prior to his 1932 hit, "Pu-Leeze, Mr. Hemingway," Kent was an architect who wrote music in his spare time. He started writing for movies in 1937 and ended up working on a total of a dozen movies, receiving two Oscar nominations.

Kent and Gannon also collaborated to write three songs for the 'Johnny Appleseed' sequence in Disney's 1948 animated feature film series "Melody Time."

Famous recording – Bing Crosby (1903-1977)

The story of "I'll Be Home for Christmas" wouldn't be complete without the mention of Bing Crosby. It was Crosby's 1943 recording of the song that made it so popular. His recording was backed by the John Scott Trotter Orchestra, and it rose to the top of the charts, remaining there for several weeks, and peaking at number three. "I'll Be Home for Christmas" became the most requested song at Christmas United Service Organizations (U.S.O.) shows in Europe and the Pacific. It was Crosby's third most successful Christmas song, the first two being "White

Christmas" and "Silent Night." The Library of Congress included Bing Crosby's rendition of "I'll Be Home for Christmas" in its National Recording Registry in 1943.

Clarifying the Credits

Early recordings of "I'll Be Home for Christmas" were credited to Sam "Buck" Ram, in addition to Kent and Gannon.

The reason for this was that Ram copyrighted a song titled "I'll Be Home for Christmas (Tho' Just in Memory)" on December 21, 1942. Of note, the song was very different from the Kent and Gannon song.

Kent and Gannon copyrighted a version of "I'll Be Home for Christmas" on August 24, 1943, then copy-righted a revised version on September 27, 1943. Bing Crosby recorded "I'll Be Home for Christmas" with the John Scott Trotter Orchestra for Decca Records on October 4, 1943.

Notable Performances and Impact

"I'll Be Home for Christmas" has been recorded by more than 250 artists worldwide. In 2014, it was named the 10th most performed holiday song by the American Society of Composers, Authors and Publishers (ASCAP). American artists who have recorded this song include Perry Como (1946), Frank Sinatra (1957), Josh Groban (2007) and Kelly Clarkson (2012). In December of 1965, "I'll Be Home for Christmas" became the first song to be broadcast into outer space by "request." Frank

Borman and James Lovell, astronauts who had just set the record for the longest flight in the US space program, were asked by a NASA transmitter if they wanted to hear any particular music as they were returning to earth. They requested Crosby's rendition of "I'll Be Home for Christmas."

Despite not being a religious song or having any reference to the birth of Christ, "I'll Be Home for Christmas" has been described as having the feel of a holiday prayer, and is often used in church programs. Its message of hope and inspiration resonates with many who may be separated from loved ones for whatever reason and long to be reunited at Christmas.

Sources

Collins, Ace. *Stories Behind the Best-Loved Songs of Christmas,* Zondervan, 2001, pp. 91-95.

https://www.independent.co.uk/news/people/obituary-walter-kent-1427740.html. Accessed July 17, 2024.

https://www.loc.gov/item/ihas.200000010/ Accessed August 3, 2024.

I'll Be Home for Christmas (hymnsandcarolsofchristmas.com). Accessed July 17, 2024.

*"I'll Be Home for Christmas" has Albany Law School Roots | Albany Law School. Accessed July 17, 2024.

Silent Night

"Silent Night" originated as a poem written in German by Joseph Mohr, an Austrian priest, just after the Napoleonic Wars. Mohr's congregation was poverty-stricken and traumatized by the ravages of war, and he wanted to convey the message that God still cared about them. The result was a six-verse poem, which includes the words:

"Today all the power of fatherly love is poured out, and Jesus as brother embraces the peoples of the world."

A poem set to music under the most unusual circumstances

While walking home one night in December 1818, Joseph Mohr looked down on the village from the top of a hill. As he took in the scenery – the snow-covered village and surrounding silence, he recalled a poem he had written a few years earlier and thought it might be appropriate for the Christmas service the next day. The only problem was that he didn't have music for it. He could probably have written the music himself, being a gifted violinist and guitarist, but instead, sought help from his friend Franz Gruber.

The next day, Mohr asked Gruber, the church organist, if he could set his poem to music. Within a few hours, Gruber had composed a melody that could be played on a guitar. That evening, they performed the new song "Stille Nacht," with Mohr playing the guitar and singing tenor while Gruber sang bass.

The various versions of this story give different reasons for why the original music was arranged for the guitar. Some sources say the organ was damaged due to rust, while others attribute the damage to mice. The story of a damaged organ has also been refuted, with the argument that there just wasn't enough time (for an organ arrangement). Whether or not it was the reason "Silent Night" was first played on the guitar, the story of a malfunctioning organ appears to have some veracity, since an organ repairman did show up after Christmas to fix the organ.

Several weeks after Christmas, Karl Mauracher came to repair the organ at St. Nicholas church, after which Mohr played the melody of "Silent Night." Mauracher was so impressed that he took copies of the lyrics and music home with him and later introduced the song to many churches and towns.

"Silent Night" spreads through Europe and America

"Stille Nacht" first became popular in the nearby Zillertal Valley, and two families of traveling folk singers - the Rainers and Strassers - started including the song in their repertoires. The Strassers learned "Stille Nacht" during their stay in a small community shortly after Mauracher had installed an organ there,

eventually spreading the song across Northern Europe. King William IV of Prussia was moved by the song's message and requested that it be performed at his annual Christmas celebration. The song spread to Eastern Europe and Great Britain, and eventually, the Rainers brought it to America.

In December of 1839, the Rainer family traveled to New York and performed "Silent Night"- in English in front of a large audience at Trinity Church. Other people began to sing "Silent Night" in churches and by the time of the American Civil War, it was the most popular Christmas carol in America.

Christmas Truce

During the US Civil War, it was not uncommon for hostilities to cease for several days around Christmas, with soldiers on both sides coming together to sing "Silent Night."

The message of peace and hope conveyed by this song is timeless and transcends national and cultural boundaries. This was demonstrated in an event now referred to as the Christmas Truce of 1914. German and British soldiers were on the frontlines in Flanders at the height of World War I; they momentarily lay down their weapons on Christmas Eve and sang "Silent Night" together.

A treasure for Austria and the world

"Silent Night" (Stille Nacht) is a national treasure in Austria, and even has five dedicated museums! While the song can be

sung at any time, public performances before Christmas Eve are discouraged and commercial use of the song is forbidden in Austria. The United Nations Educational, Scientific and Cultural Organization (UNESCO) declared "Silent Night" an intangible cultural heritage in 2011.

Creators of the Carol

Words - Josephus Franciscus Mohr (1792 – 1848)

Josephus (Joseph) Mohr became a priest by special dispensation, due to the circumstances of his birth. He grew up to be extremely generous and donated most of his income to charity. In addition to setting up a care system for the elderly, he provided funds for the education of children from poor families.

Music - Franz Xaver Gruber (1787 – 1863)

Franz Gruber was musically gifted, but his father was against his taking musical lessons. A local schoolteacher ended up giving him free music lessons secretly. Gruber eventually became a schoolteacher and church organist, and he composed several other carols.

Neither Mohr nor Gruber reaped the financial benefits of their carol that became a worldwide sensation. Fortunately for Gruber, he at least found out that his song had become a global hit while he was still alive. Unfortunately, Mohr died in 1848 without this realization.

Translation

The translation of Silent Night is usually attributed to John Freeman Young, an Episcopal priest, in 1859, even though it is sometimes listed as "Anonymous." An earlier translation, "Stilly Night," by Emily Elliot, is not well known. A British version, "Still the Night," is sometimes listed as Anonymous, even though some sources credit Stopford A. Brooks for publishing it in 1881.

The English version of "Silent Night" consists of the first, second and last verses of the original. In 1998, Bettina Klein was commissioned to create a new English translation of "Stille Nacht." Klein attempted to restore some of Mohr's original phrasing while preserving some of Young's interpretive decisions. For example, "Holy infant, so tender and mild," became "Holy infant with curly hair," consistent with the original German text. On the other hand, while *traute heilige Paar* could be a reference to Mary and Joseph (the "holy pair"), Klein retains the "mother and child" interpretation. Below is a literal translation of the first verse.

"Stille Nacht"
Deutsch (German)
Stille Nacht, heilige Nacht!
Alles schläft, einsam wacht
Nur das traute hochheilige Paar
Holder Knab im lockigen Haar,
Schlaf in himmlischer Ruh!
Schlaf in himmlischer Ruh!

"Silent Night"
English (literal translation)
Silent night, holy night
everyone sleeps; alone watches
only the close, most holy couple
blessed boy in curly hair,
sleep in heavenly peace.
sleep in heavenly peace.

Source: www.german-way.com. Accessed August 28, 2024.

Missing Verses

One of the Silent Night Museum websites provides an explanation for why verses four and five of "Stille Nacht" are less well-known. The text in these verses is not directly related to the Christmas story. For example, verse four is a celebration of freedom. The song was written at the end of the Napoleonic wars and the liberation from oppression may have been the inspiration for these words. Verse five suggests that Mohr believed that Catholic priests weren't needed to serve as mediators and redemption was to be found in God alone. Another explanation that has been offered for the "missing verses" is that verses three, four and five are difficult to sing in German.

Musical adaptation and attribution

The original melody is not quite the same as the one we recognize today and new arrangements are said to have been made for a full orchestra and organ in 1845 and 1855, respectively. When Austrian folk singers performed "Silent Night," several melody notes were altered. The Silent Night Society of Austria encourages the use of the original melody.

As "Silent Night" grew more popular, the assumption was often made that the melody had been composed by a famous musician like Mozart or Beethoven. Even though Gruber claimed the composition prior to his death in 1863, he was met with doubt. In 1995, a handwritten manuscript was found in which Joseph

Mohr had written that he composed the song in 1816, and the music was composed by "Fr. Xav. Gruber" in 1818.

From "unsuitable" to most recorded Christmas carol

Even though "Silent Night" was once considered unsuitable for inclusion in hymn books, by the late 1800s, it had been translated into over twenty languages and had become an integral part of Christmas services around the world. By the twentieth century, it had moved beyond the church into the secular world. It was first recorded by the Haydn Quartet in 1905, followed by thousands of others from around the world. "Silent Night" has now been translated into at least 300 languages.

The words of "Silent Night" have also been used for other purposes. In 1903, striking textile workers in Crimmitschau, Saxony used these words as their rallying cry: *"Holy Night, the battle rages on, work goes on, we want a little of life back!"*

Based on US Copyright Office records, "Silent Night" is the most recorded Christmas song, nearly twice as dominant as "Joy to the World."

While Mohr and Gruber didn't make money from their song, "Silent Night", they left behind a priceless legacy.

Sources

Collins, Ace. *Stories Behind the Best-Loved Songs of Christmas*, Zondervan, 2001, pp. 152-158.

Bradley, Ian (ed.) *The Penguin Book of Carols*, Penguin Books, 1999, pp. 299-302.

https://www.dw.com/en/silent-night/a-17295427. Accessed August 5, 2024.

https://folklorist.org/song/Silent_Night_(Still_the_Night,_Stille_Nacht)#google_vignette. August 6, 2024.

https://www.german-way.com/history-and-culture/holidays-and-celebrations/christmas/stille-nacht-silent-night/. Accessed August 6, 2024.

https://regency-explorer.net/silentnight/. Accessed August 6, 2024.

https://silent-night-museum.org/sounds/lyrics.htm. Accessed August 6, 2024.

https://theconversation.com/the-humble-origins-of-silent-night-108653. Accessed August 6, 2024.

https://time.com/3613551/christmas-song/. Accessed August 5, 2024.

https://www.stillenacht-wagrain.com/e_stm_start.php. Accessed August 5, 2024.

https://www.thehistoryblog.com/archives/45243. Accessed August 18, 2024.

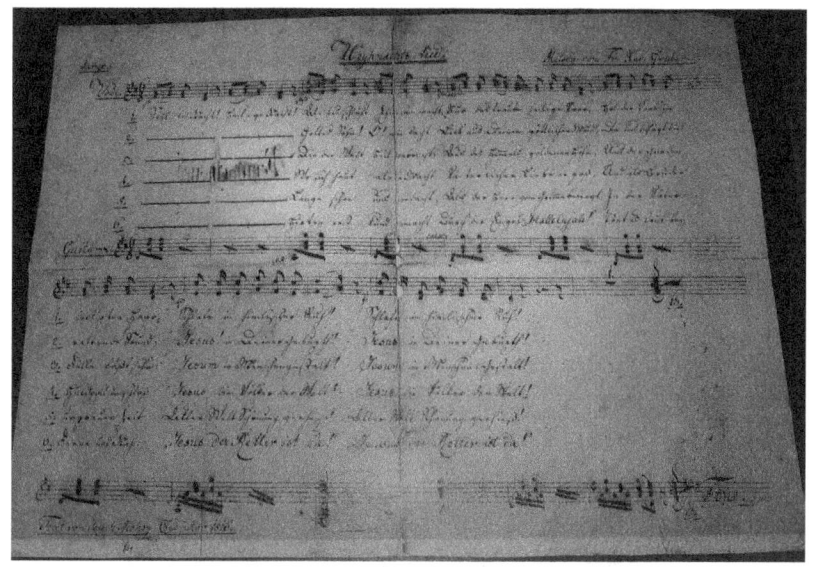

Mohr's autographed manuscript, 1820 (Silent Night Museum)

Silent Night Memorial Chapel, September 2024

The church that Joseph Mohr and Franz Gruber first performed "Silent Night" in was consecrated in 1798. The oldest building that housed St. Nicholas church in Oberndorf dates back to the 12th century. Over the centuries, parts of the building were damaged by floods and fires, with repeated attempts at restoration. The building that Mohr and Gruber performed in also fell into disrepair and had to be demolished in 1906. The people of Oberndorf wanted to commemorate the site where "Silent Night" was first performed and construction of the Memorial Chapel began in 1928. The Silent Night Chapel attracts thousands of visitors from all over the world.

Source: Silent Night Chapel

Sculpture of Joseph Mohr and Franz Gruber
outside the Silent Night Chapel

"Silent Night" is one of those songs that can make anyone stop and reflect. It's pure, it's beautiful, and it carries a message of love and hope that we all need.

– Patti Labelle, singer and actress

Silent Night

1. Silent night! Holy night!
   All is calm, all is bright
   Round yon virgin mother and child!
   Holy infant, so tender and mild,
   Sleep in heavenly peace!
   Sleep in heavenly peace!

2. Silent night! Holy night! Shepherds quake at the sight!
   Glories stream from heaven afar,
   Heavenly hosts sing Alleluia!
   Christ the Savior is born!
   Christ the Savior is born!

3. Silent night! Holy night!
   Son of God, love's pure light
   Radiant beams from thy holy face
   With the dawn of redeeming grace,
   Jesus, Lord, at thy birth!
   Jesus, Lord, at thy birth!

Stille Nacht

1. Stille Nacht, heilige Nacht,
   Alles schläft; einsam wacht
   Nur das traute hochheilige Paar.
   Holder Knabe im lockigen Haar,
   Schlaf in himmlischer Ruh!
   Schlaf in himmlischer Ruh!

2. Stille Nacht, heilige Nacht,
   Hirten erst kundgemacht
   Durch der Engel Halleluja,
   Tönt es laut von fern und nah:
   Christ, der Retter ist da!
   Christ, der Retter ist da!

3. Stille Nacht, heilige Nacht,
   Gottes Sohn, o wie lacht
   Lieb' aus deinem göttlichen Mund,
   Da uns schlägt die rettende Stund'.
   Christ, in deiner Geburt!
   Christ, in deiner Geburt!

Stille Nacht, Heilige Nacht

1. Stille Nacht! Heilige Nacht!
   Alles schläft; Einsam wacht
   Nur das traute heilige Paar.
   Holder Knab im lockigten Haar;
   Schlafe in himmlischer Ruh!
   Schlafe in himmlischer Ruh!

2. Stille Nacht! Heilige Nacht!
   Gottes Sohn! O wie lacht
   Lieb´ aus deinem göttlichen Mund,
   Da uns schlägt die rettende Stund`.
   Jesus in deiner Geburt!
   Jesus in deiner Geburt!

3. Stille Nacht! Heilige Nacht!
   Die der Welt Heil gebracht,
   Aus des Himmels goldenen Höhn
   Uns der Gnaden Fülle läßt seh´n
   Jesum in Menschengestalt!
   Jesum in Menschengestalt!

4. Stille Nacht! Heilige Nacht!
   Wo sich heut alle Macht
   Väterlicher Liebe ergoß
   Und als Bruder huldvoll umschloß
   Jesus die Völker der Welt!
   Jesus die Völker der Welt!

5. Stille Nacht! Heilige Nacht!
   Lange schon uns bedacht,
   Als der Herr vom Grimme befreit,
   In der Väter urgrauer Zeit
   Aller Welt Schonung verhieß!
   Aller Welt Schonung verhieß!

6. Stille Nacht! Heilige Nacht!
   Hirten erst kundgemacht
   Durch der Engel Alleluja,
   Tönt es laut bei Ferne und Nah:
   Jesus der Retter ist da!
   Jesus der Retter ist da!

Feliz Navidad

Singer-songwriter José Feliciano came up with "Feliz Navidad" within minutes after a producer asked him to write an original Christmas song for a 1970 holiday album. He wasn't sure he could compete with famous musicians like Irving Berlin and Brenda Lee and "Feliz Navidad" seemed too simple, but his producer liked it, and the rest is history.

Words and Music - José Feliciano (1945 -)

José Feliciano was born in Lares, Puerto Rico in 1945. His family moved to Spanish Harlem in New York when he was five. Despite being born blind due to congenital glaucoma, he showed a keen interest in music at an early age. He started playing the accordion at seven, and at eight, he picked up the ukulele after a camp experience in New York City. He then started playing the guitar around age nine or ten and then as a young teenager, started listening to records and playing from memory, since he couldn't read music. In one interview, Feliciano said braille music was "just a bunch of dots" to him. At the age of 16, he had classical training at Lighthouse for the Blind and eventually started playing in coffee houses and music clubs in Greenwich Village.

Feliciano was a hero among his fellow "Nuyoricans (New York Puerto Ricans), but his music didn't have universal appeal from the onset. RCA was initially reluctant to sign him on, so he ended up going to Argentina and performing jazz and R and B (rhythm and blues) there. When he returned to New York, RCA told him he should go back to Argentina, since he was popular there.

Feliciano did eventually get signed on by RCA, winning a Grammy for best new artist in 1968, the same year in which he performed the national anthem at the World Series. He has won nine Grammy Awards, including the LARAS Award for Lifetime Achievement. "Feliz Navidad" was inducted into the Grammy Hall of Fame in 2010.

A bilingual landmark

Feliciano wanted a song that would unite people, so he wrote "Feliz Navidad" in both English and Spanish. Working in a Los Angeles studio, he missed his family in New York and channeled those feelings into the new song. In the original version, Feliciano played the guitar and the cuatro, a ten-stringed instrument his uncle had taught him to play in Puerto Rico. The song expressed the joy he felt at Christmas and the fact that he missed his family (which included eleven brothers) and their Christmas traditions.

"Feliz Navidad" was released in 1970 but didn't catch on immediately. It didn't enter any of the US Billboard popularity charts until two and a half decades later, eventually reaching the top ten in 2020. The song has been performed by various artists, including Celine Dion and Michael Bublé.

New versions

Feliciano collaborated with Jools Holland to release a ska version of "Feliz Navidad" in 2017. (Ska is a genre of music that combines elements of Caribbean music with American jazz and rhythm and blues).

To mark its 50th anniversary, a new version of "Feliz Navidad" was recorded in 2020, in which Feliciano sang with 30 of his friends, including Jason Mraz and Gloria Gaynor. "Feliz Navidad" has been recognized as one of the top 25 most played and recorded Christmas songs worldwide by the American Society of Composers, Authors and Publishers (ASCAP).

> *"I wanted to wish you a Merry Christmas. And I think it's wonderful."*
>
> – José Feliciano

Listen Now

Thank you for reading this book! I hope you enjoyed reading as much as I enjoyed writing it! Please consider leaving an online review at the retailer of your choice. Thank you!

Olapeju Simoyan
Physician • Author
Musician • Photographer
https://thedoctorwriter.com/

Also by the Author

Books

Living Foolproof! Wisdom for Daily Living
https://mybook.to/living_foolproof

Transformation and Recovery – Lessons from the Butterfly
https://mybook.to/transformationrecovery

Giraffes are Amazing
https://mybook.to/Giraffesareamazing

The Amazing World of Butterflies
https://mybook.to/amazingbutterflies

Scranton, A Place to Call Home – The Electric City at a Glance
https://mybook.to/scranton

Essays

Where Faith and Critical Thinking Meet
https://www.patheos.com/blogs/faithandcriticalthinking/author/osimoyan/

Printed in the USA
CPSIA information can be obtained
at www.ICGtesting.com
LVHW021034021124
795374LV00009B/192